DOG WALKS AROUND THE NORFOLK COAST

By

Suzy Watson

This book is copyright material and must not be reproduced in any form except as specifically permitted in writing by the author.

All rights reserved Copyright © Suzy Watson 2016.

Maps © 2016 Suzy Watson

Updated 2020

Other publications:

Norfolk Beaches Handbook

Norfolk Heritage Walks

www.explorenorfolkuk.co.uk

Contents

Introduction 4
Map of walks along the Norfolk Coast 5
1. Snettisham (2.8 miles) 6
2. Sandringham Woods (1 or 2 miles) 9
3. Brancaster Circular Walk (4 – 4 ½ miles) 11
4. Burnham Overy Staithe Circular Walk (5.5 miles) 15
5. Wells to Holkham Circular Walk (4.5 miles) 19
6. Holt Country Park (⅓ to 1⅔ mile) 22
7. Roman Camp circular walk (3.2 miles) 24
8. Sheringham Park (3.8 miles) 28
9. Felbrigg Hall (2.7 miles) 31
10. Trimingham Cliffs (1 mile or more) 35
11. Paston Way & Pigneys Wood (3 ½ miles) 38
12. Honing Lock Circular Walk (4 miles) 42
13. Horsey Windpump (5 miles) 46
14. Winterton Dunes Circular Walk (5.3 miles) 50
15. Potter Heigham (2 or 4 miles approx.) 53
16. Mautby Marshes, Caister (5.7 miles) 57

Introduction

This Norfolk Dog Walks book was created from my own desire to find good but, more often than not, short dog walks where I could let my dogs off the lead for as long as practicably possible. I find there's nothing worse than going on a dog walk and having to keep them on the lead for ages. I would far rather they were free to enjoy themselves for as long as possible.

If you're anything like me, you want shortish walks that you can easily do in a morning or afternoon without mucking up the rest of the day.

Lots of the walks I discovered before writing this book were good for humans, but not quite so good for your four legged friend, so all these circular walks here have been tried and tested by my two Norwich Terriers, Tangle and Mutley. Although they are adorable little dogs (!) I did take into account that your pets might be a bit bigger so was very observant to make sure they were suitable for large dogs too!

These walks have minimal road walking! I've also picked walks close to the Norfolk Coast, hopefully for many visitors to enjoy. Going on holiday with your dog generally means wanting to go for walks, and trying to find good dog walks in the area you're staying in can prove to be difficult. I have tried to include walks in all the areas of the Norfolk Coast.

This book is intended to provide information only, as are the maps. We cannot be held responsible for any alterations along the paths or any loss or damage arising from your reliance of this book. **An OS map is always advisable**, although most of these walks are very obvious.

Map of walks along the Norfolk Coast

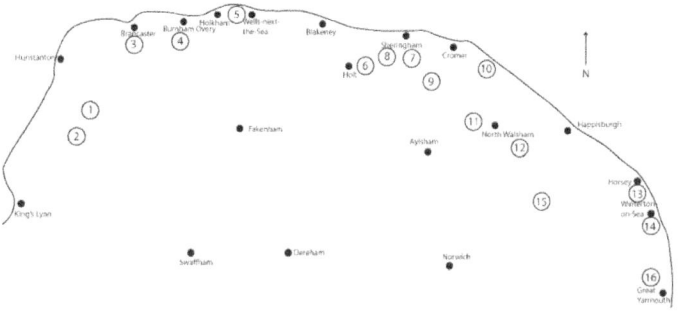

This map gives you a rough guide as to where the walks are along the Norfolk Coast.

1. Snettisham (2.8 miles)

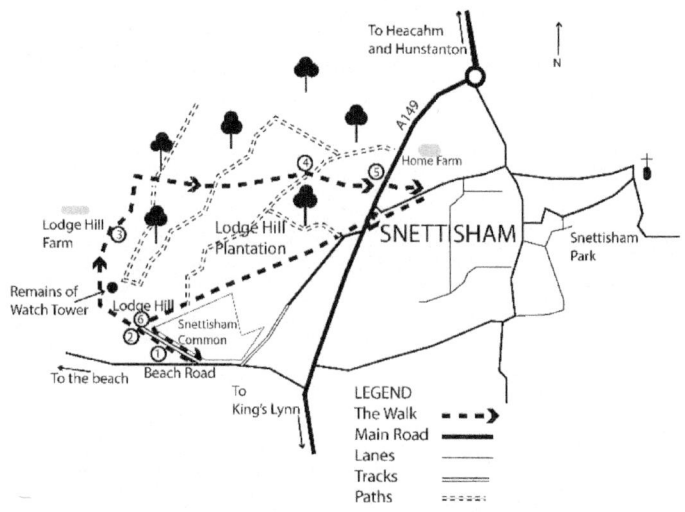

Postcode: PE31 7QY (nearest possible postcode)

What you'll see: woodland walk, views over to the Wash

Facilities: None

Length: 2.8 miles (approx. 1¼ hours)

OS Map: Explorer 250

This is a very easy circular walk through wonderful woodland which your dogs will love. There is a very small stretch where you have to cross the main road and walk along a residential road, but it is such a small part of the walk that it won't detract from the enjoyment of the rest of the walk.

1. Start at the car park just off the A149 and west of Snettisham village. To get to this car park, take the road signposted to The Beach (Beach Road) and a short way along this road you'll see the car park on the right-hand side. It isn't marked as a car park, but has a height limit barrier so you'll know when you see it. Walk away from the car park and along the short track, keeping the house on your left, until you reach a narrower but well-trodden path which takes you up into the wood.

2. Once you reach the top of the hill, head straight on through the gate (stone footpath sign on the ground). Follow the track. It is also well sign posted with green footpath signs at various intervals.

3. Once you reach another gate, you have to turn right and head on up the hill again (a very small hill!). If you look to your left as you walk up the hill, you'll see Lodge Hill Farmhouse. Continue to follow the path.

4. As you walk down the other side of the hill the path splits in two at the bottom. Take the right-hand track and you'll know you're on the right path when you see another footpath sign just after this split. Continue along here until you reach the main road. Here your dog will need to be put on the lead.

5. Cross straight over the main road, walk through the field between the fenced paddocks and you arrive

at a small residential road. Turn right here and walk back towards the main road. Once at the main road, turn left to walk along the pavement for a very short distance. Cross over to Common Road. Walk another very short distance to the corner, cross over the road and follow the footpath back into the wood (just after a 30 mph sign). Take this path all the way to the end of the wood and back to where you arrived at the stone footpath sign (No. 2 above).

6. Turn left here and head back down to the car park.

2. Sandringham Woods (1 or 2 miles)

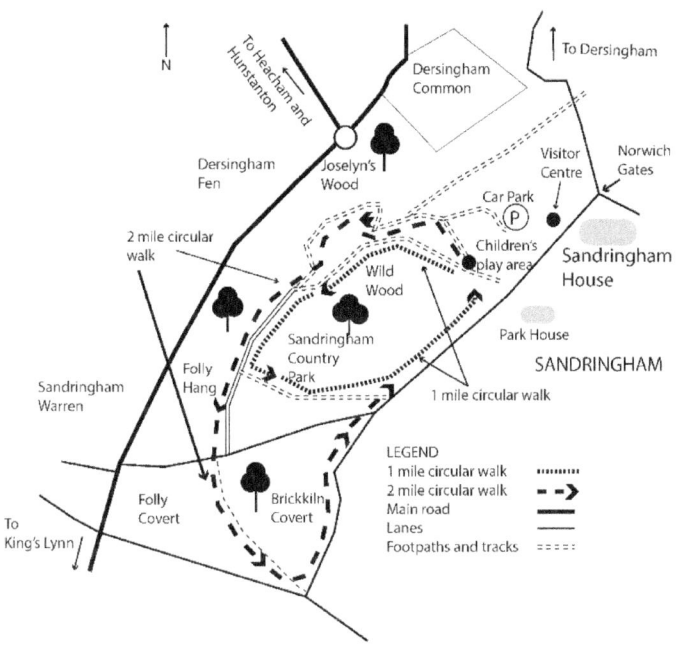

Postcode: PE35 6AB

What you'll see: Bird hide, viewing platform over to the Wash, easy gravel road walking, woodland trails, places to have picnics, Visitor Centre and shop, WC and restaurant available here

Facilities: Visitor Centre, WC's, restaurant and shop

Length: 1 mile or 2 miles (approx. 1½ hours)

OS Map: Explorer 250

Sandringham isn't just about the wonderful stately home owned by Her Majesty The Queen. It also has beautiful grounds surrounding the house, part of which is delightfully kept woodland. So these two walks are to remind you that you can visit Sandringham without entering the house and immediate grounds. These 2 circular walks give you the chance to wander amongst very picturesque woodland that is incredibly well maintained.

The two trails are very easy to follow. One is the Blue Trail which is approximately 1 mile long, the other is the Yellow Trail which says it's approximately 2 miles. They are both lovely walks.

Parking is in the Visitor Car Park which has a pay and display machine, and is well signposted. From here, walk to the enclosed children's playground, go to the far side of it, and there you will see a blue and a yellow circular sign pointing you in the direction of the walks. Both start alongside the playground and then separate a bit further along the walk.

They are really well signposted, with little circular coloured arrows attached to the trees. This is all you need to keep an eye out for!

As for leads, the only time I needed a lead was to cross the road, twice during the walk and once at the end as I neared the visitor centre. Other than that, it's a fantastic lead-free walk.

3. Brancaster Circular Walk (4 – 4 ½ miles)

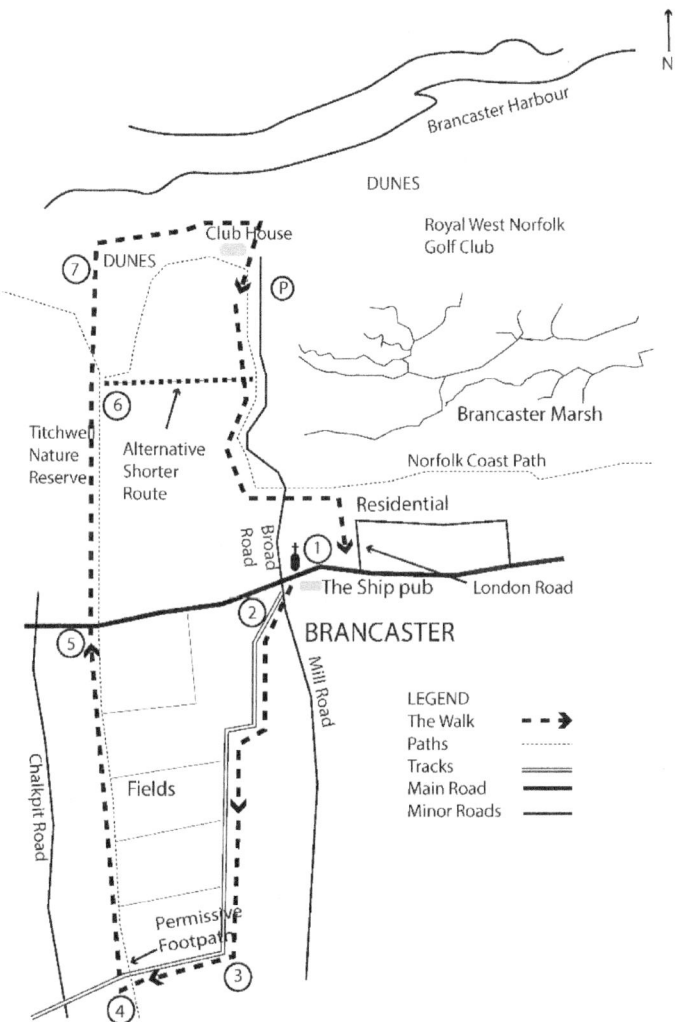

Postcode: PE31 8AP

What you'll see: walking along farm tracks and hedgerows, in amongst the reed beds and salt marshes and along the beach and sea wall. Views from the hill over towards the sea and salt marshes.

Facilities: WC at Brancaster beach car park and small kiosk

Length: From 4-4.5 miles (1½ to 2 hours)

OS Map: Explorer 250

The best thing about this walk is that it is almost all lead-free. You'll also have fantastic views over to the sea. And if you want to let your dog off the lead early on, I would suggest trying to park in Brancaster, near the church and head up for the start of the walk just opposite the church. The Brancaster Circular Walk is well signed so you won't get lost, and you don't really need a map either. However, if you don't know the area, you may not come across this walk too easily. The only slight change when on this walk (compared to the signed circular walk) is you are walking west, on the brow of the hill – here you'll come across a permissive footpath on your right heading down towards the sea (No. 4) – (the circular walk carries on here).

1. Parking can either be in Brancaster, in London Road or Broad Road, or at the Brancaster Beach Car Park which is pay and display. I'm starting this walk from the church at Brancaster. If you start here, it also means you can end up at The Ship pub for a drink afterwards! Cross the road away from

the church, heading inland, and walk along a *very small* stretch of the main road to Docking.

2. A few meters along here, take the narrow right-hand road which goes at an angle, in between flint stone houses. Follow this road which then turns into a track, all the way up to the brow of the hill. Don't forget to occasionally look behind you to get the fantastic views. Once past the houses, (about 5 mins), you'll be able to let your dogs off the lead.

3. Once you reach the top of the hill, follow the signed path to the right, along a grassy track.

4. Further along here, look out for the permissive footpath sign on the right-hand side (if you get to a small lane, Chalkpit Lane, and signposts for the Norfolk Coast Path and Peddars Way, you've gone too far). Turn right down the permissive path, keeping the hedge on your right-hand side.

5. At the bottom of the hill you'll reach the A149. Cross straight over this road and join the Brancaster Circular Walk again, heading towards the sea. Walk along the well-trodden path with hedges either side, until you come out onto the sea wall, with reed beds, salt marshes and fresh water meadows. Follow the sea wall all the way to the beach if you wish

6. If you want to make this walk slightly shorter, you can turn right along the sea wall, heading east, and

join the parallel wall which takes you back into Brancaster.

7. If you choose to carry on, head towards the beach. You can either walk over the dunes and along the beach, and then head inland once past the Club House, or you can take the path just landward of the dunes, and walk behind the Brancaster Club House. Head back towards Brancaster by walking up to the sea wall and follow this path all the way back to Brancaster village.

4. Burnham Overy Staithe Circular Walk (5.5 miles)

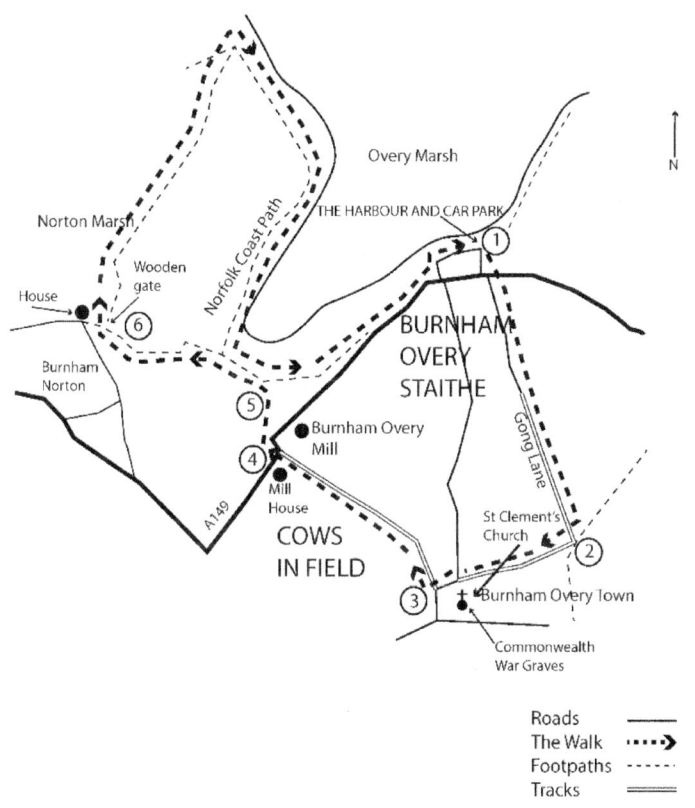

Postcode: PE31 8JF

What you'll see: The creek and quay at Burnham Overy, open countryside, The Mill and millpond, the Norfolk Coast Path and Norton Marshes. 2 stiles which larger dogs (Labrador size) can get through or around

Facilities: None

Length: 5.5 miles (just over 2 hours)

OS Map: Explorer 251

You'll also be **walking through a field with livestock** near the Mill House but the path is alongside a hedge and the cows come down into the field you walk through to get to in order to get to the river. They don't seem to be bothered by walkers, but I'll leave that to your discretion. They must be OK because there is a sign on the gate saying please keep dogs on lead, cattle in field. If they were unsure, I don't think they'd let you walk through, or put cows in that particular field.

This walk is probably the only walk that requires a bit more lead time than the other walks in this book.

I love this walk as it takes you onto the beautiful marshes on the North Norfolk Coast with endless opportunities to spot wildlife. It also starts by taking you way from the coast and onto the peaceful tracks of the countryside above Burnham Overy Staithe.

1. Park either in the car park by the creek (but beware of Spring high tide times as you don't want to come back to find your car submerged), or park alongside the creek on the verge. There are usually spaces along here. Walk away from the Quay heading towards the main road with houses on both sides of you (East Harbour Quay Road). You'll need to start this walk with dogs on leads. Walk across the main road and straight onto Gong Lane (a dead-end

road). Follow this all the way up the hill until you reach a track (take time to look behind at the beautiful views).

2. Continue along the wide track until you reach a junction of paths, with one track going straight ahead, another smaller one to the left and another one between hedgerows to the right. Take this right-hand path. At the end of this small path you reach a lane with a churchyard on your left and a smallholding on your right (you will need to put your dogs back on the lead as there are chickens here and you also reach a quiet lane).

3. Turn left onto the lane, and then at the next corner (a few paces away) turn right along another wide grassy track which takes you all the way to Mill House and the field with the cows in it. You'll also see the lovely sight of Burnham Overy Windmill. There is a stile at the entrance to this field, but the gate also opens. It's a well-trodden path which heads towards the Mill. Once through the gate at the other end, walk between the houses until you reach the A149. Cross over here and you could spend a little time at the picnic tables admiring the mill stream.

4. The next path is just on the right-hand corner of the road away from the Mill. The path is on your left with a stile. Once away from the road, the dogs can come off the leads again. Walk through this field and at the end of here you'll reach the Norfolk

Coast Path. There's another stile here too, but your dogs will be able to go through or around. Here you'll get the lovely views of the marshes, and hopefully you may hear the sound of geese flying over or see some fascinating wildlife.

5. Turn left onto the Norfolk Coast Path and you will then reach a small sign. Now, it's up to you which way you go, as this next bit is a circle. I tend to walk straight ahead along the narrower footpath but if you want to carry on along the Norfolk Coast Path, either way is good.

6. If you carry straight on, you eventually come to a house on your left and a large wooden gate on your right. Turn right, walk to the side of the wooden gate and follow the path heading towards the sea, all the way until you reach the Norfolk Coast Path again. In the winter this path can get very muddy, so boots are advised! Once on the Norfolk Coast Path, turn right and head back towards the windmill. From here you now follow the Norfolk Coast Path signs which take you diagonally across the field in the direction of the windmill and along a grassy track running parallel to the road. Now you'll need your lead again. You arrive onto the pavement of the A149. Turn left and follow the pavement, taking the first left which heads towards the harbour (a red telephone box is on the corner here). Follow this road all the way around to the right and you're back at your car.

5. Wells to Holkham Circular Walk (4.5 miles)

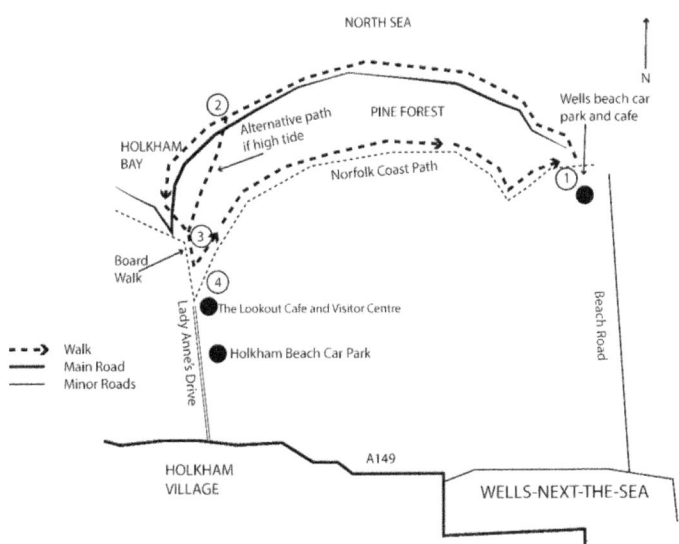

Postcode: NR23 1DR

What you'll see: Swathes of golden sand, eclectic range of beach huts, pine forests, board walk, Holkahm Bay.

Facilities: WC and café at car park and WC and café at The Lookout

Length: 4.4 miles (1 ¾ hours)

OS Map: Explorer 251

This is a walk that may seem obvious to Norfolk residents, but not so to those who don't know Norfolk.

Welly boots would be a good idea, preferable to walking boots as you may need to cross the outlet to the sea (unless you're going to be staying by the sand dunes and pine forest in which case you'll be fine without boots).

You could stop for lunch or a drink at The Victoria Inn, at the end of Lady Anne's Drive which is the Holkham beach car park or The Lookout at the top of this car park, or at Wells Beach Café on your return.

1. This walk starts at Wells Beach car park. The best place to park is at the far end of the car park as this is where the beach access is. Walk up the steps to the top of the dunes, and take in the wonderful view. Then walk down onto the beach and head west. It's entirely up to you as to how far you want to walk out on the sand, but I always like to walk as far away from the beach huts as possible. Or you can walk alongside the beach huts and hug the pine forest all the way to Holkham Bay. If the tide is right out, you can walk all the way to Holkham on the beach.

2. However, if the tide is coming in, or has just gone out, you might get stuck trying to walk over the sea inlet and channels unless you've got boots or go barefoot. So it's advisable to either check the tide times, or, quite a way further along the sand dunes you'll come across a large opening in the dunes (this is much further on from the beach huts) where

you can bear left and continue along the edge of the pine forest.

3. Once at the steps of Holkham Bay, follow the board walk until you see the beginning of Holkham Beach car park.

4. Before you reach this car park, take a sharp left along a well-trodden path which is in fact part of the Norfolk Coast Path. This is where The Lookout Visitor Centre and café is.

Continue to follow this lovely wooded walk and eventually the path opens up as you near Wells car park. Continue straight ahead, following the National Trail sign, and then bear left, with a lake and log cabins on your right. This track takes you all the way back to the car park at Wells.

6. Holt Country Park (⅓ to 1⅔ mile)

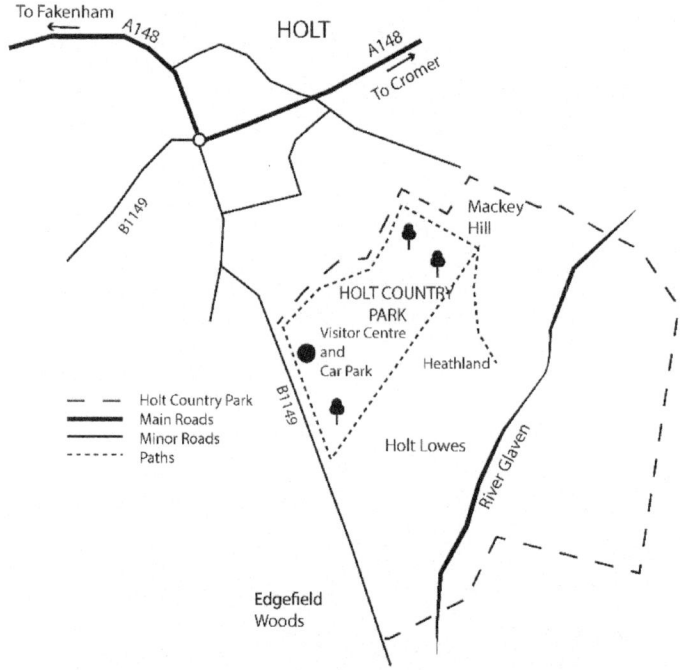

Postcode: NR25 6SP

What you'll see: Lovely woodland walk with colour coded walks, sculptures, wildlife and a playground

Facilities: Visitor Centre, WC and small tea room in the summer months

Length: Varies from ⅓ of a mile to 1 ⅔ miles

OS Map: Explorer 251

This is a relatively quiet park just outside the town of Holt which is excellent for dog walking. I haven't included any walking directions for this walk as it's a park which consists of short colour coded circular walks, so you can just arrive and see how you feel as to how far you walk. The lay of the land is flat, so it isn't difficult walking.

Outside the Visitor Centre you can pick up a leaflet which shows the circular walks. The woodland is very pretty, there are various sculptures to look out for, as well as a sensory garden.

Parking is at the entrance to the park, and there is a small charge for the whole of the day. You need to look out for the machine though, as it's fairly hidden away from view, to the side of the WC's. There is also a small visitor centre, and in the summer months a small tea room.

7. Roman Camp circular walk (3.2 miles)

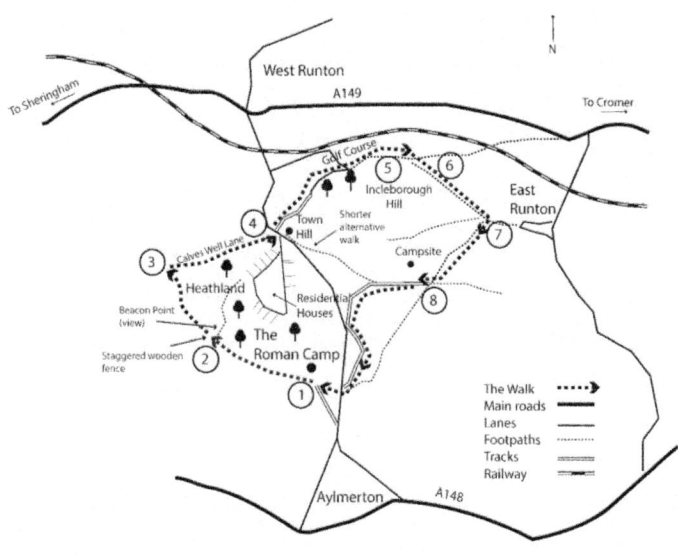

Postcode: NR27 9ND

What you'll see: Beautiful woodland, amazing views over to the sea, walking through part of the golf course

Facilities: None

Length: 3.2 miles (1 ½ hours)

OS Map: Explorer 252

Rather like the Winterton Dunes Circular walk, this is not the official Norfolk County Council circular walk. The official one is more road walking than I would like for a dog, and is also a lot longer (9.5miles). You hardly need a lead on this particular walk. In fact, for some reason, I forgot to take the leads on this walk, so that shows how much you need them, I only had to carry them for a very short way, once over a little lane and the other time a short walk through the golf course.

1. Park in the Roman Camp car park. This is just north off the A148 at Aylmerton, a turning opposite the Roman Camp Inn. Take this small lane to the T junction. Turn left and drive up the hill until you reach the Roman Camp Car Park (and National Trust West Runton and Beeston Regis Heath sign). Drive down this small track to the car park. There is a nominal 50p charge.

   Once here, take a moment to look over at the wonderful view towards the sea. There'll be a few more of these views during your walk. Take the track from the far end of the car park where you'll see a wooden post with a National Trust sign on it, as well as circular walk sign. (You can follow this circular walk sign all the way to the bottom of the hill).

2. Walk along the wide woodland track, taking in the views to your right, until you reach an opening, with the heath on your right, private property ahead and another path to your left. Take the small path just to the right of the private property sign and walk through the staggered wooden fencing. If you wish, you could take a small detour onto the heath to see the incredible views at the beacon point. Continue along the well-trodden and at times

narrow track all the way down to the bottom of the hill, keeping most of the woodland on your right.

3. Once at the bottom of the hill you'll come face to face with another staggered fence. Here the circular walk tells you to carry straight on. DO NOT carry straight on for this walk. Take the track to the right of you almost doubling back on yourself, with open fields and views of the sea to your left, and the woodland to your right.

4. Carry on all the way along here until you reach some residential houses. Here you may need to put your dogs on the lead. This track brings you out onto a lane with a small grass triangle. Straight ahead you'll see a National Trust sign saying Town Hill. If you want a much shorter walk, take this path and it will cut your walk by half.

However, for those wanting a longer walk, turn left at the grass triangle and cross over the road to the houses opposite, and along which runs the footpath (there is a restricted byway sign). Take this footpath until you reach the concrete road of the golf course. Turn left here and walk straight through the golf course along the road (dogs on leads). Beautiful views here again. This is a very short stretch of lead time.

5. Once down at the bottom of the hill, walk straight across to another narrow wooded path, keeping a picket fence on your right. As you walk along here,

you'll come across a gate saying Incleborough Hill. If you want to take a detour to the top here, you'll have amazing views over towards Cromer.

6. Carry on along this path – a little bit further on you'll come across another gate with a heavy metal wheel. If you prefer to walk along a bit of well-trodden grassy field, then go through here. Otherwise continue along the track. Both run parallel to each other. If you walk in the field, when you get to the end there's another gate which brings you back onto the path.

7. Eventually this track reaches a wooded tree tunnel with houses ahead. Look right, as here you'll see two paths. The one on the right goes almost back on yourself and up through an open field. The left hand one goes straight ahead, heading towards a radio mast. Take this left hand one and follow it all the way until you reach an opening with a campsite on your right and the paths meet at a cross roads.

8. Take the path to the right, keeping the campsite on your right, and head all the way back up the hill, through very pretty woodland, until you reach the entrance to the Roman Camp road. Cross over the road and you arrive back at the car park.

8. Sheringham Park (3.8 miles)

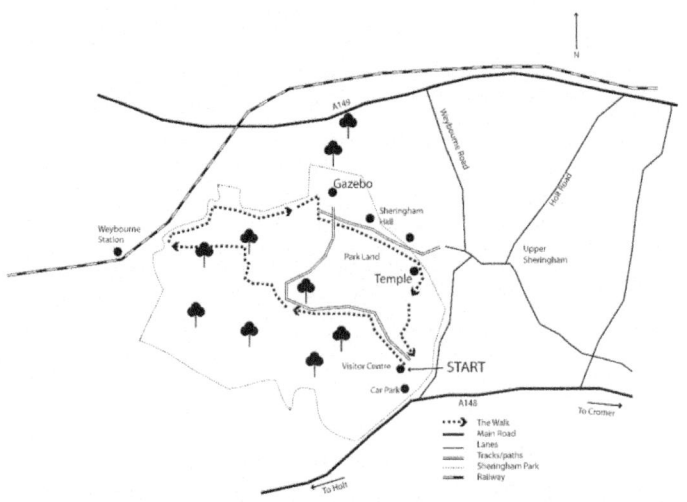

Postcode: NR26 8TL

What you'll see: this is National Trust property. Wonderful views over to the sea, the North Norfolk Railway and Weybourne Station which is also the repair yard (and possibly a steam train if you're walking at the right time), pretty woodland, beautifully landscaped parkland, a folly temple and Sheringham Hall

Facilities: At the Visitor Centre

Length: 3.8 miles (approx. 1 ½ hours)

OS Map: Explorer 252

I don't need to give you any written directions for this walk as all the walks are very well colour coded. This particular walk follows the Red Walk which is the Ramblers Walk.

From the car park, walk towards the Visitor Centre and onto the designated gravel tarmac path. Follow this until you come across the red marker on your left. This takes you left, off the main path and into woodland. The waymarkers are at very regular intervals, and whenever you wonder which way to go next, a sign will pop up.

This walk takes you alongside the North Norfolk Railway where you get amazing views to Weybourne Station. This is also the repair yard for the Poppy Line steam engines, so you may see a few of the trains out on the tracks. And if you're lucky, you'll catch a steam train going past, either on its way to Holt, or on its way back to Sheringham. This path continues, with sweeping views over to the sea, and then takes you into more woodland before emerging into to parkland of Sheringham Park. All of these are excellent dog walking paths.

Just before you reach the parkland, if you look up onto the top of the trees ahead, you'll see the gazebo. If you have time, it's definitely worth walking to the top of it, as the view is beautiful.

Continuing on the walk, you'll now pass Sheringham Hall, in all its splendour, and walking on the tarmac Sheringham Park path towards Hall Farm and up to the folly temple on the right-hand side, again another wonderful view over to Sheringham Hall and the sea.

From the temple, you walk behind and down into the field. Following the red arrows takes you down to the bottom of a field with gorse on the right-hand side and a fence on the left until you reach a gate at the bottom which brings you to a farm track and eventually back onto the tarmac paths of Sheringham Park. Turn left and head back towards the car park.

9. Felbrigg Hall (2.7 miles)

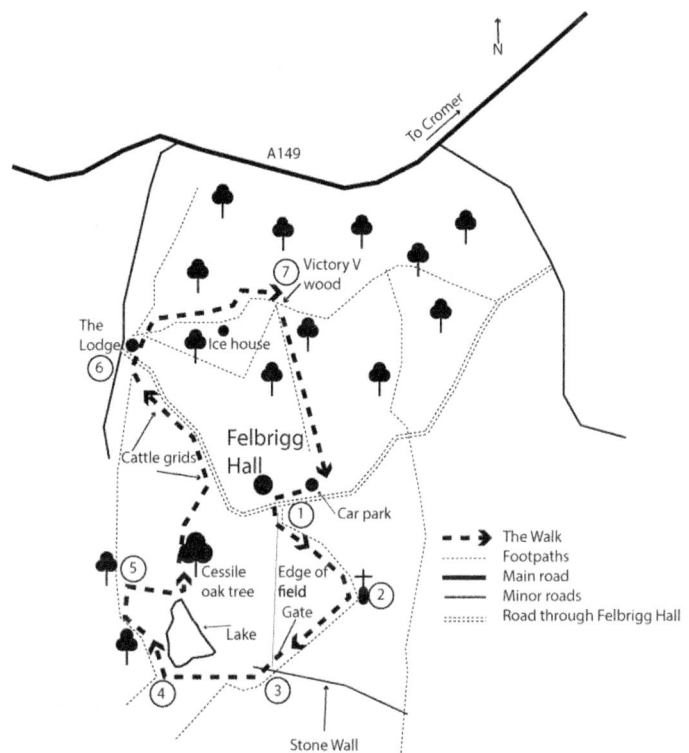

Postcode: NR11 8PR

What you'll see: Felbrigg Church (with unusual box pews), Felbrigg Lake and the woodlands and ice house. The Victory V wood, Felbrigg Hall and the Walled Garden (dogs not allowed in here)

There is every possibility that there will be sheep in at least one of the fields you walk through, so this is probably the only time you will need a lead (particularly if your dogs are prone to running around)

Facilities: WC and café but best to check for opening times. Parkland is open all year round

Length: 2.7 miles (approx. 1 hour)

OS Map: Explorer 252

1. Start at the Felbrigg Hall National Trust car park (a charge applies). If you park at the near end, furthest away from the Hall, and look to your left, you will spot a wooden gate into parkland and the church ahead of you. This is the gate you want to walk through to start your walk. It is also signposted for the Church Walk and Lakeside Walk. Head towards the church.

2. Once at the church, walk through the wooden gate ahead of you (keeping the church on your left), and enter into a large field. Take the 45 degree well-trodden path straight up through the field to the top of the hill.

3. Once at the top of the hill you'll be met by a kissing gate. Here, look right and take a look at the splendid view over to the Hall. Go through this gate, turn left and head towards the stone wall. Go through the open gate and turn immediately right, heading down towards the lake, keeping the wall on your right. There are benches beside the lake where you could rest and admire the view.

4. Head to the end of the lake and turn immediately right, don't go straight on. Walk through the woodland keeping the lake on your right. Eventually you arrive at another gate with a Weaver's Way sign. Follow this for a short distance up the hill until you come out to a clearing by an oak tree. Then you are slightly left to work out which way to go!

5. Turn right and head down towards another part of the lake and in the direction of the Hall. Walk through the gate and across the bridge (more Weaver's Way signs), turn left and continue along this path until you reach yet another gate! Half way along this path you'll come across the huge Cessile Oak tree. (If you wanted to walk back to the Hall from here, there is a gate behind this tree which takes you back to Felbrigg Hall).

Continuing on along the path, once through the gate, you can either go straight ahead (which brings you out at a cattle grid) or bear slightly right and follow the path to end up at the tarmac road. Turn left and walk on along this tarmac road, over 2 cattle grids until you almost reach The Lodge house.

6. Just before The Lodge, turn right into the woodland and follow the path, signed with a red arrow, all the way to the Victory V Wood (which has a bench circling one of the trees and a sign to tell you about

the wood). You'll also walk past an ancient ice house here as well.

7. Once at the Victory V wood, take the left-hand wide path, all the way back down to the Hall, passing the walled garden on your left, and the car park is straight ahead. You will need to put your dogs on the leads at the very end here.

10. Trimingham Cliffs (1 mile or more)

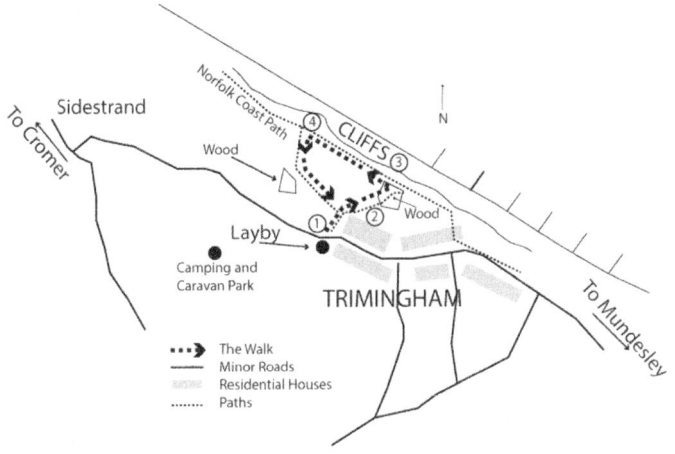

Postcode: NR11 8QJ

What you'll see: Woodland, cliff tops and wonderful views towards Overstrand and Mundesley. *Please note that you can't get down to the beach from Trimingham, this is merely a cliff walk*

Facilities: None

Length: 1 mile (or more, depending on where you want to walk to (just under 1 hour). You could just do a linear walk to Sidestrand

OS Map: Explorer 252

This walk can be any length you wish. As you walk along the cliff tops, you may want to carry on further towards

Sidestrand and Overstrand and then double back on yourself once you feel you've gone as far as you want.

The views from the cliffs are fantastic. Coastal erosion is very evident here, so you need to be fairly careful about walking too close to the edge. You may want to keep your dogs slightly under control during parts of this walk as the cliff can be a bit precarious in places.

1. Parking - as you approach Trimingham from the north, there is a wide layby on the left-hand side, just before you reach the residential houses. You should be able to park here. Walk towards the end of the layby nearest the houses and turn left towards the sea, keeping the hedge on your right.

2. Follow the well-trodden path diagonally right through the field towards a small wood. Once in the wood, there are various paths you can take.

3. Keep to the left-hand path and walk out of the wood at the far top left end. There are Norfolk Coast Path markers dotted in the wood. Once out of the wood you'll see the cliffs ahead of you to your left. Walk along here for as long as you like.

4. About a quarter of the way along the cliffs you'll see a wooden signpost saying restricted byway (pointing back towards the main road). If you want a circular walk, take this path, up the slight incline and towards another small wood. Follow the track to the corner of the field you started off at, so

bearing slightly left once at the wood. (If you carry straight on along the grassy track towards the road, you'll end up a little bit further along from where you parked).

11. Paston Way & Pigneys Wood (3 ½ miles)

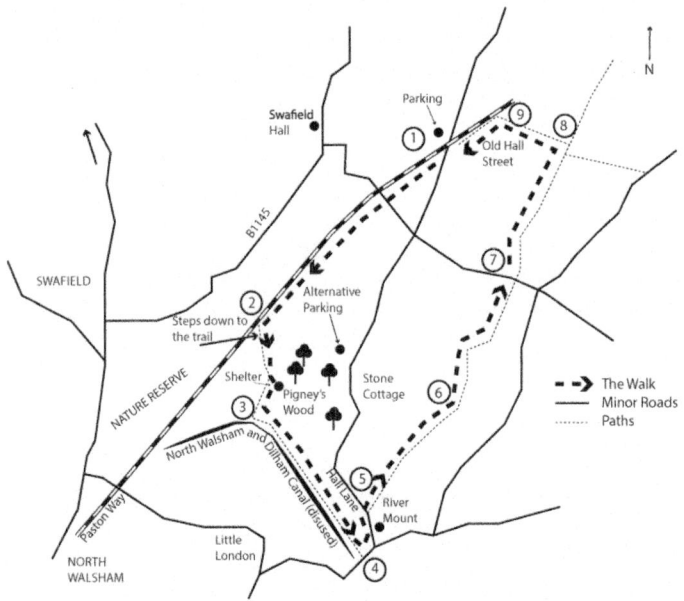

Postcode: NR28 0SB (this takes you to the alternative visitor car park which you don't want. So, **continue** to drive north a short distance and you'll come across the car park in Old Hall Street – see the note before the route directions)

What you'll see: Woodland, walking along an old disused railway that is now part of the Paston Way walking trail, walking alongside the disused North Walsham and Dilham Canal, a nature reserve and open fields and countryside

Facilities: None

Length: 3.4 miles (just under 1 ½ hours)

OS Map: Explorer 252

This is quite a diverse walk in that one minute you'll be walking in woodland and through a nature reserve, the next you'll be wandering along a disused canal and onto open countryside.

The car park is a bit tricky to find, but head north out of North Walsham towards Old Hall Street (you will probably need a map for this). There are two car parks fairly close together, one is an obvious picnic site and Pigneys Wood car park. You don't want this one, continue north for a little further and you'll come across another small car park opposite some houses. Park here.

1. Once in the car park you'll see some wooden steps down to the old disused railway line which is part of the Paston Way. Walk all the way along this path, under the bridge, until you reach some wooden steps on the left which takes you down to a lower part of the wood. Walk down these steps to the information board.

2. This information board tells you all about the Pigneys Wood trails. There are 3 different coloured walks you can take, but this particular walk follows part of the yellow trail (only part of it!) Follow the yellow trail to the right of you (as you're looking at the board). This take you along a narrow wooded path until you reach a clearing. Now here, although the yellow trail says go right, all this does is take

you around the side of the field. It's easier to walk straight ahead, where you'll see a shelter with picnic tables and posters about the wildlife hanging on the walls.

3. Turn right at the shelter and walk along the high sided bank and nature reserve. Walk straight ahead until you reach the canal. Once at the canal, turn left and follow this all the way to a small lane.

4. You'll need a lead here, but only for a very short while. Turn left onto the lane, and left again onto Hall Lane, and walk along here until you reach a metal gate the far side of River Mount House.

5. If you look in the hedge you'll see a footpath sign. Walk along this footpath, up the hill along the wide grassy track with the field on your left and keeping the hedge on your right.

6. At the top of the hill, turn right and then left (signposted) and carry on walking alongside the fields and then cutting right through a field just before a road. This is the footpath.

7. Once at the road, you cross over and head along the small wooded path, signposted and very obvious. Walk all the way along this path until you spot a sign for the Paston Way and a tall gas pipeline marker on the right.

8. Keep going, but only for a short while and keep your eyes open for another sign and a hole in the hedge on the left.

9. Walk through this hole, across the field until you reach a house hidden behind a tall garden hedge and a wire fence. Again, it's very obvious and is part of the Paston Way. Turn left along the hedge and fence until you reach a small lane. Opposite here is the car park.

12. Honing Lock Circular Walk (4 miles)

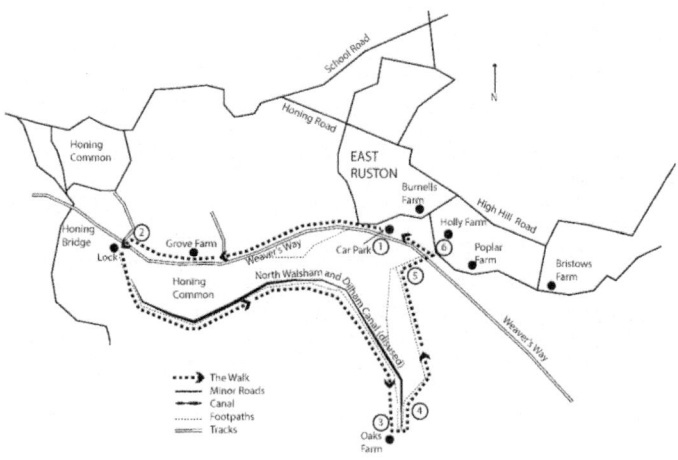

Grid Ref: TG346272

What you'll see: Woodland, walking along an old disused railway that is now part of the Weavers Way walking trail, walking alongside a large part of the disused North Walsham and Dilham Canal, open fields and countryside. Sheep may be in a couple of the fields, and if it's been wet, it can get quite muddy so boots or walking boots are definitely advisable! **Hardly any lead needed at all except maybe if there are sheep in the field.**

Facilities: None

Length: 4 miles (approx 1 ¾ hours)

OS Map: Explorer 252

This is a really pretty walk alongside the North Walsham and Dilham Canal which is now disused, as is the railway line that you'll also walk along and forms part of the Weavers Way.

Park at the Weavers' Way car park, just at the south of East Ruston village. This walk is well signposted as the "Honing Lock circular walk".

1. Step onto Weavers Way and turn right and follow this straight disused railway line, through three gates, passing the East Ruston Angling Club on your left.

2. Once through this third gate you'll notice a signpost. Follow the sign for Honing Lock Circular Walk which takes you slightly to the left and off the Weavers Way. Head towards a small wooden footbridge and continue a very short way until you reach Honing Lock. Once you get here you'll see the old brick canal (such a pity it isn't working today). Walk over the bridge and turn immediately left and follow the canal all the way until you can go no further. Before you reach this point, you'll walk through marsh and meadows which may have sheep in and very pretty woodland right alongside the canal as well as walking over a few wooden footbridges. It's all very well signposted and just remember to keep the canal on your left at all times.

3. Eventually the walk arrives at a hedge with a gate, and a house opposite (this hedge and gate is very

obvious). Walk through this gate and turn immediately left to walk over the brick bridge going over the canal. You are now going to walk back on yourself (on the opposite side of the canal) for a short while.

4. After the 2nd gate that you walk through, take the path to the right (again well signposted with post and wire fences on either side). Follow this path between the marshland all the way until you almost reach a house.

5. Just before you reach the house you'll see a gate on your right hand side which is again signposted with a low stile. Look out for this one. Walk straight across the field to the other side where you then walk over a wooden footpath and find yourself back on the Weavers Way.

6. Turn left here and walk a short distance back to the car park.

13. Horsey Windpump (5 miles)

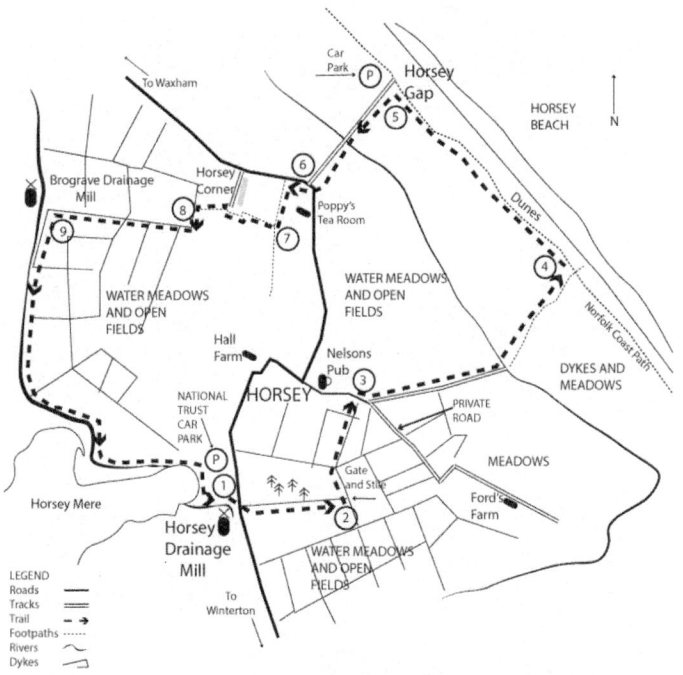

Postcode: NR29 4EF

What you'll see: Seals on the beach if you walk in winter, sand dunes, Brograve Drainage Mill and Horsey Windpump, marshes and reedbeds, Horsey Mere, meadows, farmland, WWII pill box on dunes. (Charge for car parking)

Facilities: WC in the National Trust Car Park

Length: 5 miles (approx. 2 ½ hrs depending on how long you may take watching the seals)

OS Map: Explorer OL40

There may be livestock in the first field so you will need to keep your dogs on a lead and under control. You'll also need to keep them under control if you're looking at the seals, and there is one other very small bit of road walking where you'll need to put them on a lead.

Horsey Windpump is one of those particularly attractive sights as you drive along the very typical Broads straight but undulating road. It's owned by the National Trust and you can also pay to go up the windpump too.

1. Park at the National Trust Horsey Windpump car park where there are WC's and a little National Trust shop selling refreshments. Cross over the road and followed the fairly well-trodden path heading towards the sand dunes in the distance with the wood on your left. Walk along this field until you come to a dyke (there may be livestock in this field during certain times of the year, but you keep to the edge of the field anyway).

2. Turn left, over a stile (dogs can go around to the right), walking alongside the dyke and towards a tarmacked road.

3. Once you reach this road, turn right and then take the left-hand fork, again towards the sea. This fork was badly signposted but there is a polite notice to say you are trespassing if you go the wrong way!

You may also see a damaged sign saying "private road"! From here you take the track all the way to the dunes and arrive at the sea defences. If you do this walk in the winter, the entrance to the beach will be closed off for the seals and their pups. You can take a small detour to the right along the dunes to arrive at the viewing platform specifically constructed for seal watching, and what a sight it is!

4. However, to continue on the walk, once you reach the beach you turn left and can either walk along the back of the dunes in the winter, or on the beach in the summer months, passing the old WWII pill box with incredible views for miles, until you arrive at Horsey Gap car park.

5. Continue left out of the car park and continue to the main road.

6. Turn right along the main road, (here you will need a lead), and continue for about 100 meters where you then take a footpath (signposted) to the left through the field.

7. At the end of this short field by a hedge you turn right towards a small cluster of houses. Follow that path which brings you out onto a small narrow lane. Almost immediately, you turn left along another signed footpath keeping a house on your left, and walk out towards open land.

8. Once you reach a dyke, cross over a wooden flat footbridge and head towards the old relic of Brograve Drainage Mill. Brograve Drainage Mill is an opportunity for a photograph! It's a fantastic former windpump and it's just how you might imagine a watercolour or oil painting of the Norfolk Broads.

9. Once at the mill, turn left and follow this path, walking alongside the large dyke, with reeds to your right and open countryside to your left. This path eventually takes you past the side of Horsey mere and back to Horsey Windpump and the car park.

14. Winterton Dunes Circular Walk (5.3 miles)

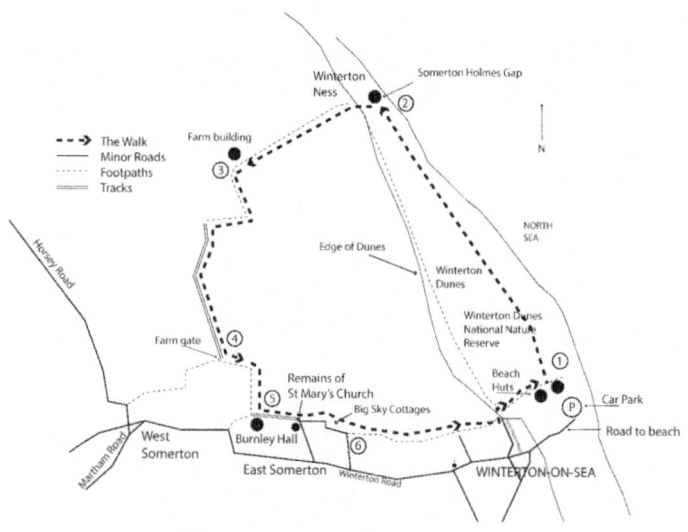

Postcode: NR29 4AJ

What you'll see: An amazing expanse of sand dunes, farm tracks, an old church ruin

Facilities: WC and café at the car park

Length: 5.3 miles (approx. 1 ¾ hours)

OS Map: Explorer OL40

This walk entails a very short stretch where you dog will need to be on the lead.

This isn't the official Norfolk County Council Winterton Dunes circular walk as that walk takes you along the roads of Winterton, this one doesn't. This walk is slightly "observing the masses and doing the opposite"!

1. Park in the Winterton Beach car park. There is a parking attendant and the cost varies as to how long you'll be staying. Drive to the far end by the wooden huts as this is where the walk starts. Walk through the huts and head out north-west along the dunes and along the well-trodden paths (or the beach if you prefer). There are lots of paths criss-crossing the dunes, but all you need to do is head north west, walking parallel to the sea. You'll walk up and down the dunes, but keep going for approx. 1.7miles. **Early on you'll come across a circular walk sign, don't follow this**, just keep straight on. It's up to you which paths you take, but eventually you reach a small copse of low trees.

2. Follow the path until you eventually arrive at Somerton Holmes and Gap. This has a concrete sea defence going down to the beach, so it's very obvious when you arrive at it. From here, take the path heading inland, walking through concrete boulders and along a wide farm track. You eventually arrive at a farm building.

3. Turn left here and take the footpath which takes you along the edge of a field. Follow this track until you reach a concrete road (a concrete boulder will tell you you've arrived). Walk along this track all the way until you meet a metal farm gate.

4. Walk around this gate and turn left (keeping the impressive wall of Burnley Hall on your right) and walk along this road until you reach the old church ruin.

5. From here you'll need to put your dogs on the lead for a very short while. Once past the church, walk straight ahead, passing a couple of houses on your right, and Big Sky Cottages on your left.

6. Follow the road around until you reach another grassy farm track. Here you can take the dogs off the lead. Follow this track, heading in the direction of Winterton church. This track takes you all the way to Winterton. Depending on how well behaved your dogs are, you may need to put them on the lead a little bit further along here, but not for long. Walk past houses and allotments and you will arrive at North Market Road.

7. Turn left here and you'll see that straight ahead you'll be back on the dunes. You'll be able to let them off the lead again! Head right and back to the car park.

15. Potter Heigham (2 or 4 miles approx.)

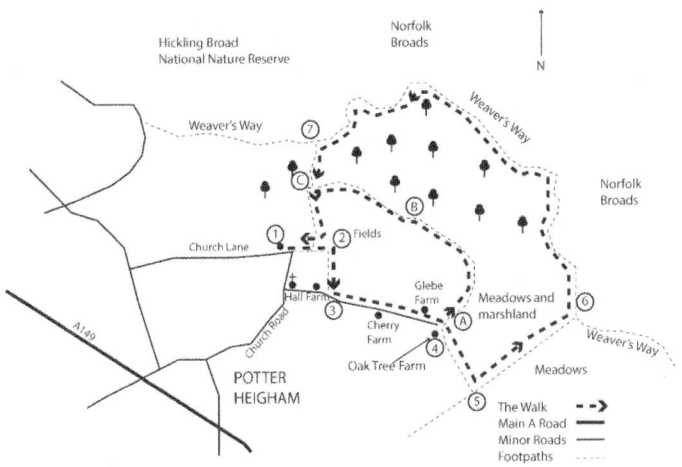

Postcode: NR29 5LL (Nearest postcode I can get)

What you'll see: marshland and reedbeds, the broads landscape, dykes, woodland and wildlife, Konik ponies

Facilities: None

Length: 1.88 miles (approx. ¾ hours) or 3.7 miles (approx. 1 ½ hours)

OS Map: Explorer OL40

These are two walks which start in the same place, one is along the broads and Weaves Way, the other is amongst the woodland just inland from Weaver's Way. Both need very little time on the lead.

1. To park, drive past the church on your right, and carry on until you reach a sharp left-hand corner. Park here at this corner on the verge. You'll see the footpath sign. Walk along the edge of the field keeping the hedge on your right.

2. At the end of the hedge, walk INTO the field, to a small marker post (not far) and turn right and head towards the houses. This is the footpath. Once you reach the houses, you'll see the gap where you come out onto the road.

3. Turn left onto the road which is a dead-end so it's very quiet. This is the only place you'll need the lead. Walk along here for about 0.4 miles, until you reach the end house, Oak Tree Farm, and the road ends.

4. *This is where you go left for Walk 1 and right for Walk 2.*

For Walk 1 (1.88 miles)

A. Take the track on the left which is signposted. Follow this farm track all the way to the wood. Don't go through any gates on your right. Keep going until you come across what looks like a dead end. (A gate on your right and a wood in front of you).

B. Here you'll see a small but very well-trodden path. Follow this narrow path, through the wood, and eventually you'll be walking alongside the dyke which is on your right. Continue along here. The dyke eventually heads off away to your right.

C. Continue along this path until you come to a wider opening and another path on your right with a sign saying Hickling Broad Nature Reserve (this is where the longer Walk 2 joins), and a path on your left. Take this path to the left, walk all the way along here until you reach the hedge, turn right and you're back at your car. Hardly any time on the lead!

For Walk 2 (3.7 miles)

Start as for Walk 1 all the way to Oak Tree Farm and take up from point No 4 above. When you reach Oak Tree Farm, turn right along the farm track as far as you can go until you come to a metal gate.

5. Turn left here and follow the track until you reach a right-hand corner, passing marshland meadows and dykes on both sides. Just at this corner is a small footbridge (signposted Weavers Way) which takes you up onto Weavers Way. Go over this bridge.

6. Turn left to follow this Weavers Way trail and continue along this path, following swathes of reedbeds on your right and woodland and water on your left. You may well see the Konik ponies in the woods (the Norfolk Wildlife Trust and Broads Authority are protecting the special interest of Hickling by grazing with this breed of pony). This

path continues, passing open broads, a bird hide and eventually a signpost pointing in both directions for the Weavers Way.

7. At this signpost, turn left and walk into the woodland. Continue in this direction until you reach a T junction path (as in C above). Turn right and then left, and head back to your car.

16. Mautby Marshes, Caister (5.7 miles)

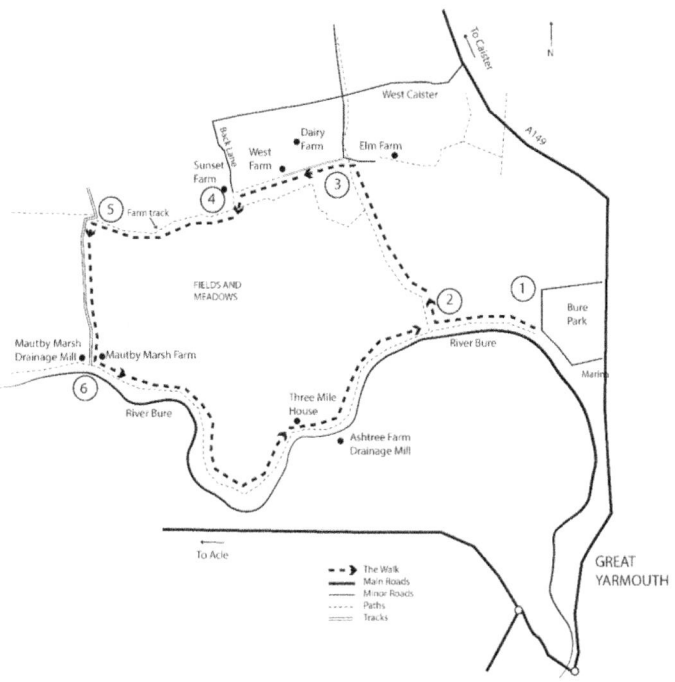

Postcode: NR30 4AS

What you'll see: Marshland and reedbeds, fields, a windmill, walking along the raised bank of the River Bure.

Livestock may be near the river, but they just move away when you reach them. Please keep your dogs under control when you see the livestock. This is a slightly different walk to the Norfolk County Council Mautby Marshes circular walk3

Facilities: None

Length: 5.7 miles (approx. 2 hours)

OS Map: Explorer OL40

This is a pretty walk alongside the raised bank of the River Bure, part of the Norfolk Broads. Depending on what time of year you take this walk, you'll undoubtedly see a boat or two motoring slowly along.

1. Park at the Bure Park car park, just off the main A149 heading into Great Yarmouth. Don't stop at the first small car park, drive on to car park near the pitch and putt. Start the walk by heading towards the playground and the River Bure. Once you've reached the river, turn right and follow the well-trodden path all the way to the signpost which is signed for Mautby circular walk. HOWEVER, unless you want a much longer walk, do not follow all these circular signs as the Norfolk County Council circular walk takes you a long way from the marsh.

2. Turn right at the sign post and follow the signs until you reach some houses (you can go the other way but I prefer to finish the walk along the riverside).

3. When you reach the houses, there is a signpost pointing left that says Bridleway and another sign saying No Vehicular Access. Turn left here along a gravel track, passing a handful of houses on your right, and follow this path through a small wooded area until you reach another house and farm in front of you (Sunset Farm).

4. Turn left here into the fields (it is a footpath), heading in the direction of the river (ignore the circular walk signs pointing you in the opposite direction as this takes you on a long detour). Once past the first small field, turn right and take this path along the edge of the field for as far as you can go, which is to a dyke. The path bears left and then right (this track is used by farm tractors) and this will eventually bring you out onto a tarmac road.

5. Turn left here and walk towards the Mautby drainage mill and farm, as well as the river.

6. Once you reach the river bank, turn left and follow the path all the way back to the car park.

Printed in Great Britain
by Amazon